Before They Were President

BEFORE BARACK OBAMA WAS PRESIDENT

Gareth Stevens
PUBLISHING

By Julia McDonnell

Please visit our website, www.garethstevens.com. For a free color catalog of all our high-quality books, call toll free 1-800-542-2595 or fax 1-877-542-2596.

Library of Congress Cataloging-in-Publication Data

Names: McDonnell, Julia, 1979- author.
Title: Before Barack Obama was President / Julia McDonnell.
Description: New York : Gareth Stevens Publishing, 2019. | Series: Before they were president | Includes index.
Identifiers: LCCN 2018022958| ISBN 9781538229095 (library bound) | ISBN 9781538232484 (pbk.) | ISBN 9781538232491 (6 pack)
Subjects: LCSH: Obama, Barack–Juvenile literature. | Obama, Barack–Childhood and youth–Juvenile literature. | Presidents–United States–Biography–Juvenile literature. | Legislators–United States–Biography–Juvenile literature. | United States. Congress. Senate–Biography–Juvenile literature. | Presidents–United States–Election–2008–Juvenile literature. | United States–Politics and government–2001-2009–Juvenile literature.
Classification: LCC E908 .M394 2019 | DDC 973.932092 [B] –dc23
LC record available at https://lccn.loc.gov/2018022958

First Edition

Published in 2019 by
Gareth Stevens Publishing
111 East 14th Street, Suite 349
New York, NY 10003

Copyright © 2019 Gareth Stevens Publishing

Designer: Laura Bowen
Editor: Therese Shea

Photo credits: Cover, p. 1 (Obama) Official White House Photo by Pete Souza/Jatkins/Wikimedia Commons; cover, p. 1 (Harvard campus) Jannis Tobias Werner/Shutterstock.com; cover, pp. 1–21 (frame) Samran wonglakorn/Shutterstock.com; p. 5 Pete Souza, The Obama-Biden Transition Project/Hoshie/Wikimedia Commons; pp. 7 (family photo), 9 Barcroft/Barcroft Media/Getty Images; p. 7 (Hawaii) Izabela23/Shutterstock.com; p. 11 Laura S. L. Kong/Hulton Archive/Getty Images; p. 13 EQRoy/Shutterstock.com; p. 15 (main) Steve Liss/The LIFE Images Collection/Getty Images; p. 15 (inset) Official White House Photo by Chuck Kennedy/Jatkins/Wikimedia Commons; p. 17 Malcolm Ali/WireImage/Getty Images; p. 19 Spencer Platt/Getty Images News/Getty Images; p. 21 (family) Everett Collection/Shutterstock.com; p. 21 (Obama) United States Senate/Movieevery/Wikimedia Commons.

Printed in the United States of America

CPSIA compliance information: Batch #CW19GS: For further information contact Gareth Stevens, New York, New York at 1-800-542-2595.

CONTENTS

Words in the glossary appear in **bold** type the first time they are used in the text.

THE 44TH PRESIDENT

"You can be anything you want to be when you grow up—even president!" Has anyone ever told you that? Perhaps Barack Obama also heard—and believed—those words when he was young!

Did Obama always dream of being elected president? Or did his life turn out in ways that surprised him? What hopes, jobs, and events turned him into the man who made history as the first African American president? Read on to find out—and start dreaming big, too!

Presidential Preview

Barack Obama's name sounds like: buh-RAHK oh-BAH-muh. "Barack" means "blessing" in the African language of Swahili.

BARACK OBAMA WAS 47 YEARS OLD WHEN HE WAS ELECTED THE 44TH PRESIDENT OF THE UNITED STATES. HE WAS THE FIFTH-YOUNGEST US PRESIDENT.

5

HAWAIIAN BEGINNINGS

Barack Hussein Obama was born in Honolulu, Hawaii, on August 4, 1961. His mother, Ann Dunham, was white and originally from Kansas. His father, who was also named Barack Obama, was black and from the African country of Kenya. His parents met as students at the University of Hawaii and married in February 1961.

When his parents **divorced** in 1964, Barack stayed with his mother. After she got married again, the family moved to his stepfather's home country of Indonesia in Southeast Asia.

Presidential Preview

Obama is the only US president born in Hawaii.

YOUNG BARACK AND FAMILY

THIS PHOTO SHOWS BARACK (RIGHT), HIS MOTHER, HIS STEPFATHER LOLO SOETORO, AND HIS HALF-SISTER MAYA.

HONOLULU, HAWAII

CHILDHOOD OVERSEAS

While living in Indonesia's capital city of Jakarta, Obama became familiar with different **cultures**, languages, **religions**, and foods. He said, "I was raised as an Indonesian child and a Hawaiian child and as a black child and as a white child."

Obama went to local schools at first. After a few years, his mother sent him back to Hawaii to get a better education. He lived with his grandparents Stanley and Madelyn. He called them "Gramps" and "Toot."

Presidential Preview

While Obama was in Indonesia, his family had an ape named Tata and even raised crocodiles!

BARACK OBAMA IS PICTURED WITH HIS THIRD-GRADE CLASS IN INDONESIA IN THIS PHOTO FROM 1970.

9

QUESTIONING HIS IDENTITY

As one of only three black students at Honolulu's Punahou School, Obama became more aware of his skin color. Though he's **biracial**, others saw him as black—and blacks often weren't treated as well as whites. His mother encouraged him to be proud to be black, but Obama didn't feel connected to his African roots. He only saw his father one more time after his parents divorced.

Young Barack used the nickname "Barry." He later said he felt **confused** about who he was and where he fit in during his teenage years.

Presidential Preview

During high school, Obama worked at an ice cream shop. He said it taught him about **responsibility** and hard work.

As a teenager, Barack dreamed about playing basketball professionally. Some teammates called him "Barry O'Bomber." He loved taking hard shots—but often missed them.

11

LIFE ON THE MAINLAND

After graduating from high school, Obama left Hawaii again. He went to Occidental College in Los Angeles, California, for 2 years and then switched to Columbia University in New York City. There, Obama earned a **degree** in political science, which is the study of governments and how they work.

After school, Obama became a writer for a business journal in New York City. He enjoyed writing, but decided he wanted to do something else with his life.

Presidential Preview

Obama is distantly related to seven US presidents: James Madison, Harry Truman, Lyndon Johnson, Gerald Ford, Jimmy Carter, George H. W. Bush, and George W. Bush.

OBAMA'S INTEREST IN POLITICS BEGAN AT OCCIDENTAL COLLEGE. HE SAID HE LEARNED THAT HIS "VOICE COULD MAKE A DIFFERENCE." DURING HIS TIME THERE, HE DECIDED TO BE CALLED "BARACK."

OCCIDENTAL COLLEGE

A HOME IN CHICAGO

Obama moved to Chicago, Illinois, in 1985 to serve as a community organizer in the city's South Side. His job was to direct efforts to improve poor neighborhoods. He had some successes but decided he could make more of a difference as a lawyer. He began Harvard Law School in 1988.

After finishing school in 1991, Obama returned to Chicago. In 1992, he married a lawyer he'd met through a summer job at a law firm. Her name was Michelle Robinson.

Presidential Preview

In 1987, Obama visited Kenya to learn more about his father, who had died in 1982.

OBAMA WAS THE FIRST BLACK PRESIDENT OF THE *HARVARD LAW REVIEW,* A JOURNAL THAT STUDIES LEGAL MATTERS.

MICHELLE ROBINSON OBAMA

15

MAKING A DIFFERENCE

Obama practiced civil rights law. Civil rights are the freedoms that all citizens should have. Obama said he fought "on behalf of families who are having a tough time and are seeking out the American dream." He also directed an effort to increase the number of African American voters and taught at the University of Chicago Law School.

Through these jobs, his interest in politics grew. He thought serving in the state **legislature** would be a way to help bring about change.

Presidential Preview

For a time, Obama held three jobs: state senator, lawyer, and teacher.

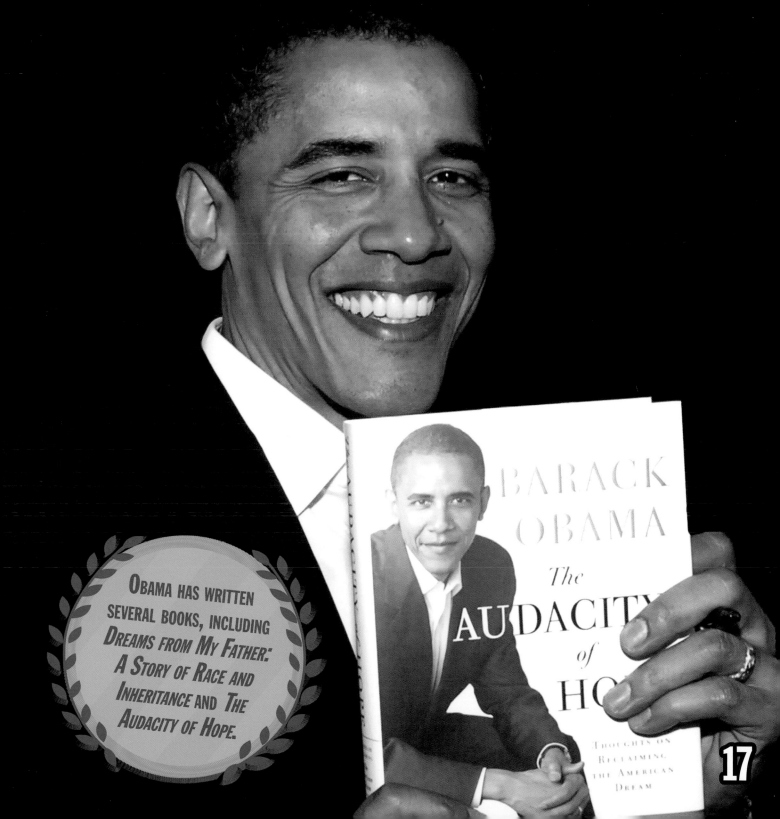

OBAMA HAS WRITTEN SEVERAL BOOKS, INCLUDING *DREAMS FROM MY FATHER: A STORY OF RACE AND INHERITANCE* AND *THE AUDACITY OF HOPE*.

DREAMING BIGGER

In 1996, Obama became the Democratic **candidate** for a seat in the Illinois State Senate. He won and served for 8 years, focusing on better health care and education. He ran for US Senate in 2004.

Before the election, Obama gave a speech at the Democratic National **Convention**. Millions of people watching on TV liked his positive message about America. He was called "a rising star" in government. Obama won his election and became the fifth black man to serve in the Senate.

Presidential Preview

Obama ran for a seat in the US House of Representatives in 2000 but lost. However, he gained experience that helped him win later elections.

Obama talked about having hope for the future in his speech during the Democratic National Convention of 2004. He also said, "There's not a black America and white America and Latino America and Asian America; there's the United States of America."

VICTORY!

In 2007, Barack Obama announced he was running for the highest office in US government. He promised to work for change in health care, education, and financial matters. On November 4, 2008, he beat Republican candidate Senator John McCain to become the president.

Obama once talked about himself as "a skinny kid with a funny name who believes that America has a place for him, too." Obama's place turned out to be the White House! His story is an example of how hard work and big dreams can take you far.

Presidential Preview

Obama's **campaign** used the sayings "Hope" and "Change We Can Believe In."

Obama's Road to the Presidency

1961 Barack Obama is born in Honolulu, Hawaii, on August 4.

1967 He moves to Indonesia.

1971 He returns to Hawaii to attend school.

1979 He finishes high school and begins to attend Occidental College.

1983 He receives a degree in political science from Columbia University.

1985 He moves to Chicago to work as a community organizer.

1987 He visits Kenya and meets his father's family.

1991 He receives a law degree from Harvard.

1992 He returns to Chicago and marries Michelle Robinson.

1993 He starts work at a law firm.

1996 He's elected to the Illinois State Senate.

2004 Obama is elected to the US Senate.

2008 Barack Obama becomes US president.

OBAMA FAMILY, ELECTION NIGHT 2008

PRESIDENT OBAMA

21

GLOSSARY

biracial: having a mother from one racial group and a father from another

campaign: a series of activities to reach a goal, such as to win an election

candidate: a person who is trying to be elected

confuse: to mix up

convention: a large meeting of people who come to a place for usually several days to talk about work or other interests or to make decisions as a group

culture: the beliefs and ways of life of a group of people

degree: a statement and title given to someone who has completed a program of study at a college or university

divorce: to end a marriage

legislature: a lawmaking body

politics: the activities of the government and government officials

professionally: having to do with earning money from an activity that many people do for fun

religion: a belief in and way of honoring a god or gods

responsibility: the quality of a person who can be trusted to do what is expected or required

FOR MORE INFORMATION

Books

Obama, Barack. *Of Thee I Sing: A Letter to My Daughters.* New York, NY: Alfred A. Knopf, 2010.

Orr, Tamra B. *Obama vs. McCain and the Historic Election.* Ann Arbor, MI: Cherry Lake Publishing, 2018.

Souza, Pete. *Dream Big Dreams: Photographs from Barack Obama's Inspiring and Historic Presidency.* New York, NY: Little, Brown and Company, 2017.

Websites

Barack Obama
www.whitehouse.gov/about-the-white-house/presidents/barack-obama/
Read Obama's official presidential biography.

Kid Reporter Interview: Obama on Being the President
www.scholastic.com/teachers/videos/teaching-content/kid-reporter-interview-obama-being-president/
Watch a young reporter ask Obama why he liked being president.

INDEX